MACMILL/

PRE-INTERM

L. FRANK BAUM

The Wizard of Oz

Retold by Elizabeth Walker

MACMILLAN

MACMILLAN READERS

PRE-INTERMEDIATE LEVEL

Founding Editor: John Milne

The Macmillan Readers provide a choice of enjoyable reading materials for learners of English. The series is published at six levels – Starter, Beginner, Elementary, Pre-intermediate, Intermediate and Upper.

Level control
Information, structure and vocabulary are controlled to suit the students' ability at each level.

The number of words at each level:

Starter	about 300 basic words
Beginner	about 600 basic words
Elementary	about 1100 basic words
Pre-intermediate	about 1400 basic words
Intermediate	about 1600 basic words
Upper	about 2200 basic words

Vocabulary
Some difficult words and phrases in this book are important for understanding the story. Some of these words are explained in the story and some are shown in the pictures. From Pre-intermediate level upwards, words are marked with a number like this: ...[3]. These words are explained in the Glossary at the end of the book.

Answer keys
Answer keys for the *Points for Understanding* and the *Exercises* sections can be found at www.macmillanenglish.com

Contents

A Note About The Author

Lyman Frank Baum was born in 1856 near Syracuse, in New York State, in the Eastern part of the United States. His father made a lot of money in the oil business and Frank grew up with his brothers and sisters in a beautiful house in the countryside.

Frank was not a healthy child. He had a weak heart, so he could not play games like other children. But Frank enjoyed reading and he also liked writing his own stories and telling them to his friends.

When Frank was fifteen years old, he started a newspaper. At the same time, he also became very interested in the theater. Frank's father owned several theaters and he asked his son to manage one of them. Frank wrote a play for this theater and he played the leading part himself.

In 1882, Frank married Maud Gage. Although Frank and Maud were very different, their marriage was a happy one and they had four sons.

Frank continued to work very hard and his health became worse. He joined his father's business, but that later failed and most of the money was lost.

Frank and his family moved to the Midwest in 1882 and in 1888 he opened a shop called "Baum's Bazaar". The shop was very popular, but it only lasted two years. People in the Midwest were poor and they could not afford to buy very much. Frank went on to manage a weekly newspaper, but this also failed.

After this, Frank worked as a reporter on a newspaper, and then as a traveling salesman, in Chicago.

Although Frank worked very hard, he always had time to tell his stories to his children. He decided to write stories for other children, too. A few years later, he began to publish these stories and his books of fairy tales became very popular. Frank had at last found the work that he could do best.

L. Frank Baum's most famous book was *The Wonderful Wizard*[1] *of Oz*, which was published in 1900. The book made Frank a great deal of money. In 1908, he was able to move his family to California, where they lived in a house called "Ozcot". Frank Baum wrote many more books about Oz. These include *Ozma of Oz* (1907), *The Road to Oz* (1909), *The Lost Princess of Oz* (1917), and *Glinda of Oz* (1920). But *The Wonderful Wizard of Oz* has always been his most popular book.

Frank lived his last years in California, and he finally died from several illnesses in May 1919. He had worked very hard all his life and his health was never good. But his books have brought pleasure and delight to thousands of readers—children and adults alike.

A Note About This Story

L. Frank Baum wrote many books about the land of Oz, but *The Wonderful Wizard of Oz* is his most famous. Most people know its story because of the 1939 film which is titled "The Wizard of Oz", starring Judy Garland. Because of the lasting fame of the film, we have called this Reader *The Wizard of Oz*, rather than *The Wonderful Wizard of Oz*.

However, the film "Wizard of Oz" is different from Baum's book in several ways. *The Wonderful Wizard of Oz* is an American folk tale. But its witches and beasts[2] are not as frightening as the ones in the European tales of the Brothers Grimm. The story is based on the "American Dream"—that anyone can do anything if they believe in themselves. And that the simple pleasures of home are better than the strange and exotic[3].

The heroine is the brave and sensible Dorothy, who lives with her Aunt Em and Uncle Henry in a little house on the gray Kansas[4] prairie[5]. Their life is hard and simple, but Dorothy is happy to help her aunt and play with her little dog, Toto.

Then a cyclone[6] comes and Dorothy and Toto are blown away to the magical Land of Oz. Dorothy loves the colorful landscape[7] and people, but the story is about her wish to go home.

But Dorothy's journey back to Kansas will be long and difficult. She learns that only one person may be able to help her, the Great Wizard of Oz. She must follow the yellow brick[8] road to the Emerald City, where Oz lives. When she gets there, she must ask Oz for his help.

As she travels along the yellow brick road, Dorothy meets a Scarecrow[9], who wants brains, a Tin[10] Man who wants a heart, and a Lion, who wants to be brave. Although Oz cannot really help them, Dorothy and her friends get what they want because they have self belief.

The film, starring Judy Garland as Dorothy, is still very popular today. In the film, the strange characters that Dorothy meets are people she knows in her "real" life. The Land of Oz is also just a dream. In the book, Oz is as real as Kansas. And in the film, the Silver Shoes become red slippers. This is because red shows better on the cinema screen than silver!

Some people have seen political ideas in the book. It is true that Oz tricks his people as cleverly as a politician. Every part of the Land of Oz has its own color and people have seen political ideas in that too. *The Wonderful Wizard of Oz* can be read by people at any age. It can be as simple or as complicated as the reader wants it to be. And that is why L. Frank Baum's masterpiece is still enjoyed today.

BEASTS → bestie o animale

The People in This Story

Dorothy

Scarecrow

Tin Man

Cowardly Lion

Aunt Em

Uncle Henry

The Wizard of Oz

The Wicked Witch of the West

Glinda, the Good Witch of the South

Toto

1

The Cyclone

Dorothy lived in the State of Kansas with her Uncle Henry and her Aunt Em. They all lived in a little wooden house in the middle of the great Kansas prairie. The land was very flat and there were no trees or other houses nearby.

Uncle Henry was a farmer and he had built the wooden house himself, many years before. The house only had one room. That room was used for eating and for sleeping in too.

There was a little hole under the house that was called the "cyclone cellar". The family hid in the cellar when the strong winds of a cyclone blew across the prairie.

The hot sun had burnt the paint on the little house. Now the paint on the house was gray. The sun had burnt the land around the house too. Everything on the prairie was gray. Uncle Henry and Aunt Em had gray hair and gray, tired faces.

Dorothy's Uncle Henry and Aunt Em were poor and they had worked very hard all their lives. It was not easy to be a farmer on the prairie and Uncle Henry was always very tired. He never smiled and Aunt Em always looked sad too. But Dorothy was always laughing. The girl had a little black dog called Toto. Dorothy played with Toto all day long.

But today, Dorothy and Toto were not playing. Uncle Henry was standing with Dorothy in the doorway of the little house. He was looking at the gray sky and he was very worried. Then they heard the sound of a strong wind. It was coming from the south. It whistled[11] and roared[12]. It blew the long grass of the prairie until it was flat.

"There's a cyclone coming, Em!" Uncle Henry called to

his wife. "Get into the cyclone cellar! You get in too, Dorothy. I'll look after the cows and horses."

"Quick, Dorothy! Get inside!" Aunt Em cried as she opened the wooden trap door to the cellar.

Aunt Em climbed down through the trap door into the little hole. Dorothy ran into the house with Toto. But the little dog was afraid of the wind. He jumped down from Dorothy's arms and ran under her bed. Dorothy caught him quickly and ran back across the room. But it was too late. The wind had blown into the house and shut the trap door. Dorothy could not get into the cyclone cellar. The wind blew harder and harder. The little house shook and Dorothy fell down onto the floor.

Then a strange thing happened. Uncle Henry and Aunt Em's house began to move. It turned around and around and went up and up. It was in the center of the cyclone where the north and south winds met. The winds pushed the house higher and higher, like a balloon[13].

The little house was carried over the prairie for miles and miles. Many hours went by. It was very dark now and the wind went on making its terrible roaring sound. At last Dorothy lay down on her bed with Toto beside her. The girl closed her eyes and she was soon fast asleep.

Hours later, Dorothy was woken up by a hard bump[14]. Everything had gone still. The house had stopped turning and bright sunshine filled the room with light.

"Quick, Dorothy! Get inside!" Aunt Em cried as she opened the wooden trap door to the cellar.

2

In the Land of the Munchkins

Dorothy jumped down from her bed and ran to the door. When she opened it, she gave a cry of surprise.

She was not looking at the gray prairie anymore. The house was in a beautiful country that was covered with green grass and tall trees. There were flowers of every color in the grass and the trees were full of delicious fruit. Birds sang and there was a little stream of clear water.

"How different this country is from Kansas!" Dorothy cried. "I have never seen such a beautiful place. Where am I? And how did I get here?"

At that moment, Dorothy saw some people coming towards her. The people were small, but they were not children. The three men had beards and the woman's hair was white.

They were all very strangely dressed. They wore blue hats that were tall and pointed. The men were all dressed in blue, but the little woman was dressed in white. She walked towards Dorothy and bowed[15].

"Welcome to the Land of the Munchkins," the woman said. "Thank you for killing the Wicked[16] Witch of the East. You must be a witch too. You have killed the Wicked Witch with your magic[17] and now we are free. Thank you."

Dorothy was very surprised. She had no magic and she had never killed anyone in her life.

"You have made a mistake," Dorothy replied. "I am a girl, not a witch. I have not killed anyone."

"Well, then your house killed her. It fell on top of her," said the woman with a laugh. "Look, you can see the legs of the Wicked Witch sticking out from under the house. You can see her Silver Shoes."

"Oh, dear," Dorothy said, looking down at the witch's legs and the beautiful Silver Shoes on her feet. "What can I do?"

"Nothing," the little woman said. "The Wicked Witch of the East is dead. I am the Good Witch of the North, my dear. I am the Munchkins' friend and now yours too."

Dorothy was very surprised.

"I thought that all witches were wicked," she said slowly.

"No, that's not true," the Good Witch of the North replied. "There were four witches in the Land of Oz—two were good and two were bad. But now, thanks to you, there is only one wicked witch—the Wicked Witch of the West. There is a wizard too. He is the Great Wizard of Oz and he lives in the Emerald City."

"I am a girl and I live in Kansas with my aunt and uncle," Dorothy replied. "Well, I used to live with them," she went on sadly. "I was carried here by the cyclone and now I want to get back to Kansas. Can you help me?"

The Good Witch shook her head.

"There is a desert[18] all around the Land of Oz," she said. "No one can cross it. You will have to stay with us, my dear."

Dorothy began to cry.

"This is a beautiful country," she said. "But Kansas is my home. Uncle Henry and Aunt Em are there and they will be worried about me. Home is always the best place to be. Please help me to go home."

The girl went on crying and the Munchkins began to cry too, because they felt sorry for her. The Good Witch of the North thought for a moment.

"You must go to the Emerald City," she said after a while. "The Great Wizard of Oz lives there. Ask him to help you."

"How do I get to the Emerald City? Is it a long way? Will you come with me?" Dorothy asked.

"You must follow the yellow brick road," the Good Witch

replied. "It is a long way. But my kiss will protect[19] you. No one will hurt you when they see this mark[20]."

The Good Witch kissed Dorothy and smiled. The kiss had left a strange mark on Dorothy's forehead.

"Go to the Great Wizard. You will be safe now," she said.

Dorothy stopped crying and thanked the Good Witch.

"Look, the Wicked Witch has turned to dust!" one of the Munchkins said to Dorothy. "Take her Silver Shoes, my dear. They may help you on your journey. Goodbye."

The Munchkins walked away through the trees, talking happily. The Good Witch of the North smiled and walked away too.

Dorothy and Toto were all alone in the Land of Oz.

3

Dorothy Meets the Scarecrow

Dorothy was feeling hungry. She went into the house and found some bread. She gave some bread to Toto and ate some herself. Then she picked some fruit and drank some water from the stream.

A clean blue and white dress was hanging by Dorothy's bed. The girl washed herself carefully and put on the dress. Then she put some more bread in her basket. She picked some more fruit and put that in the basket too.

Dorothy looked down at her shoes. They were old and dirty. Then she looked at the Wicked Witch's Silver Shoes.

"I will wear them if they will fit me," she said to herself, and she put them on. Toto barked[21] loudly and wagged[22] his tail.

"Come along, Toto," Dorothy said. "We will go to the Emerald City and see the Wizard of Oz. This is a beautiful country, but I must get back home to Kansas."

The brave girl picked up her basket and shut the door of the house behind her. Then they started on their journey.

Soon they found the yellow brick road and walked along it happily. There were fields on both sides of the road. All the houses that Dorothy saw were painted blue—the Munchkins' color.

In the evening, Dorothy was very tired and she wanted somewhere to sleep. Then she saw a large Munchkin house. It was painted blue, like the other Munchkin houses. But this house belonged to a very rich Munchkin. He had invited his friends to supper and the food was on two long tables in front of the house. Music was playing and the Munchkins were all dancing on the grass.

The rich Munchkin looked at Dorothy's Silver Shoes.

"You are young, but you must be a very good witch," he said.

"Why?" Dorothy asked in surprise.

"You are wearing the Silver Shoes. They belonged to the Wicked Witch of the East. This means you have killed her," the Munchkin explained. "Please eat with us. Your little dog can have some food too. And I have a room where you can sleep."

After her supper, Dorothy was very tired. She was taken into a room where everything was blue. The bed was very soft with blue sheets. Dorothy and Toto fell asleep at once.

When Dorothy woke up, breakfast was ready for her. After she had eaten, the girl asked the Munchkin a question.

"How far away is the Emerald City where the Wizard of Oz lives?" she asked. "I want to see him."

"The Wizard never sees anyone," the Munchkin replied. "And many people are frightened of him. It is a long way to the Emerald City and the journey will be dangerous."

"But I want to get home to Kansas and the Great Wizard is the only one who can help me," Dorothy said bravely. "So I must go to the Emerald City. Goodbye and thank you."

And Dorothy and Toto started on their journey again.

After they had walked several miles along the yellow brick road, Dorothy sat down to rest. There was a big cornfield by the side of the road. In the middle of the field was a Scarecrow. It was fixed onto a pole[23].

The Scarecrow's head was made from a sack[24] which was stuffed[25] with straw[26]. He had two painted blue eyes, a nose, and a mouth.

Dorothy looked at the Scarecrow and smiled.

"We have scarecrows in Kansas too," she said. "They scare

the crows and stop them eating the corn."

"That's right," the Scarecrow said.

Dorothy looked at the Scarecrow in surprise.

"But our scarecrows in Kansas don't talk," she said.

"I don't talk much," the Scarecrow replied. "I'm standing here because I can't get down. The crows are not scared of me. They have brains and I don't."

"Oh dear," Dorothy said kindly. "Perhaps I can help you."

She stood up and lifted the Scarecrow down from the pole. He was dressed like a Munchkin, in blue clothes.

"That's better. I can move my legs now," the Scarecrow said. "What is your name, my dear? Where are you going?"

"My name is Dorothy. I am going to the Emerald City to see the Great Wizard of Oz. I want to go home to Kansas."

"The Emerald City? The Wizard of Oz? Kansas? I don't know anything about these things because I have no brains," the Scarecrow said sadly. "My head is stuffed with straw."

"Well, Kansas is my home," Dorothy said. "And there is no place like home, you know. The Wizard of Oz lives in the Emerald City. He is very clever. I hope that he can get me back to Kansas."

"Do you think that Oz would give me some brains?" asked the Scarecrow.

"I don't know," Dorothy replied. "Why don't you come with me and ask him?"

"Thank you," the Scarecrow said. "That is a good idea."

As they began to walk, Toto barked at the Scarecrow. The little dog had never seen a straw man before.

"Don't be afraid. Toto won't bite you," Dorothy said.

"I'm not afraid," the Scarecrow replied. "I'm only afraid of one thing."

"What is that?" asked Dorothy.

"Fire," the Scarecrow replied.

They walked all day. In the evening, they came to a great forest. It was dark under the trees, but the yellow brick road went on into the darkness. Dorothy could not see and she held the Scarecrow's arm.

"I must rest soon. I have been walking all day," she said.

"Well, I feel sorry for you. I never get tired, because I have no brains," the Scarecrow replied. "I can see a little house under the trees. Shall we stay there tonight?"

"Yes, please," Dorothy said. She went inside the little house and fell asleep at once. Toto was soon asleep too. The Scarecrow, who never got tired, stood by the door all night.

4

Dorothy Helps the Tin Man

When Dorothy woke up, the Scarecrow was waiting by the door. Toto was running around and barking, and there was sunlight shining through the trees.

"I must find some water," Dorothy said to the Scarecrow. "I need to wash and drink. The bread in my basket is very dry."

"I am made of straw, so I don't need water," the Scarecrow said. "You are made of flesh[27] so your life is more difficult than mine. But you have brains and you can think."

"You will soon have brains too," Dorothy said kindly.

They continued on along the yellow brick road and came to a stream. Dorothy washed and drank, and Toto drank too.

Suddenly, they heard a shout.

"Who's that?" Dorothy cried. Then she saw something shining under the trees and gave a cry of surprise. It was a man made of tin! The Tin Man had an axe[28] in his hands, but he did not move at all.

"Can I help you?" Dorothy asked the Tin Man.

"I hope so," the Tin Man said. "I am a woodman[29]. I was working here when it rained. My joints[30] rusted[31] and I couldn't move. My oil can[32] is in my house. Please get it for me."

Dorothy ran back to the little house and found the oil can. She poured oil over the Tin Man's joints. First, the Tin Man moved his neck, then he moved his arms. Last of all, he moved his legs.

"That is much better," he said. "I have not been able to move for a year and my axe is very heavy. Not many people come this way. Where are you going?"

"We are going to the Emerald City, to see the great Oz,"

Dorothy replied. "I want to go home to Kansas with Toto, my dog. I hope that the Wizard can help me. My friend, the Scarecrow, will ask Oz to give him some brains."

"I have no heart," the Tin Man said sadly. "Could Oz give me a heart?"

"Why don't you come with us and find out?" Dorothy asked.

The Tin Man thought for a while. Then he said,

"Thank you, I will. Please put my oil can in your basket. I will need it if it rains."

So the friends went on their way along the yellow brick road. Soon, the trees became very thick. Then the Tin Man was a great help. He cut the trees with his axe and made a path[33] for them all.

"You must have brains," the Scarecrow said. "Because you know how to make a path through the trees."

"I used to have brains and a heart," the Tin Man replied. "Now I have neither. Do you want to know why?"

Dorothy and the Scarecrow nodded.

"When I was a man of flesh," the Tin Man said, "I loved a Munchkin girl, but her mother hated me. She asked the Wicked Witch of the East to put some magic in my axe."

"That was very bad of her," Dorothy said.

"Every time that I used my axe, it slipped," the Tin Man went on. "First, it cut off my left leg, then it cut off my right one. I asked a tinsmith[34] to make me new legs and I went on with my work. Then, the magic axe cut off both my arms. So I asked the tinsmith to make me new arms. Then I cut off my head, so he had to make me a new head. But when my body was cut in half, I lost my heart. Now I cannot love anymore."

"Brains are better than a heart," the Scarecrow said

Dorothy did not answer. She had brains and a heart, but she could not get back to Kansas. She was worried too. The bread in her basket was nearly all gone. Her new friends did not need food. But she did, and so did Toto.

5

The Cowardly[35] *Lion*

The yellow brick road went on through the forest and Dorothy was becoming a little afraid.

"How big is this forest?" the girl asked the Tin Man. "Are we far from the Emerald City?"

"I don't know," the Tin Man replied. "There may be wild animals living here, but don't worry. Animals don't eat straw or tin. You are made of flesh, but you are safe because the good Witch has kissed you."

"But what about my dog, Toto?" Dorothy asked.

At that moment, they all heard a terrible sound. It was the roar of a Lion! Then the Lion ran onto the road and knocked over the Scarecrow.

With another roar, the Lion knocked over the Tin Man too.

Toto was very brave. He ran up to the Lion, barking loudly. The Lion opened his mouth.

"No, no!" Dorothy shouted and she hit the Lion on his nose. "How dare you! You coward[36]! How dare you bite a poor little dog!"

"I didn't bite him. I only opened my mouth," the Lion said. "I am a coward and I am afraid of everything. When I roar, my heart beats very fast because I have no courage[37]."

"At least you have a heart," the Tin Man said. "I don't. I am going to ask the Wizard of Oz for one."

"You have brains too," the Scarecrow said to the Cowardly Lion. "I don't. But I am going to ask the Wizard of Oz for some."

"Toto and I want to go home to Kansas. I am going to ask Oz to help us get back there," Dorothy said.

"Do you think that Oz can give me courage?" the Cowardly Lion asked. "Then I wouldn't be a coward anymore."

"The Wizard of Oz is very powerful," Dorothy replied. "You are welcome to come with us and ask him."

And so they went on their way. The Scarecrow carried Dorothy's basket and the Cowardly Lion walked by her side. Toto was afraid of the huge animal at first, but they soon became friends.

That night, they had to sleep in the forest. The Tin Man cut down a tree and made a fire with the wood. Dorothy and Toto ate the last of their bread.

"There is no food for breakfast," Dorothy said.

"I can kill an animal for you," the Cowardly Lion told her. "Then you can cook it on the fire."

"I think that it is wrong to kill anything," the Tin Man said. "But as I have no heart, I am not sure."

The Cowardly Lion did not answer. He went into the forest and was away for some time.

The Scarecrow found a nut[38] tree and he picked some nuts.

"Put them in your basket, my dear," he said to Dorothy. "You can have them for breakfast. Now you and Toto must sleep. I will stand under this tree, away from the fire."

Dorothy and Toto slept well. In the morning, the girl ate the nuts and drank some water from a stream. Soon, all the friends were walking along the yellow brick road again.

It was not an easy day. After a time, they came to a very wide ditch[39]. The ditch divided the forest in two and it was too wide to cross. Dorothy walked to the edge of the ditch and looked into it.

"We can't climb down there," she said. "The ditch is too deep and there are rocks[40] at the bottom. What can we do?"

The Scarecrow and the Tin Man looked at each other, but they did not speak. The Cowardly Lion walked to Dorothy's side and looked across the ditch.

"I think that I could jump over it," the Cowardly Lion said at last.

"Then you can carry us on your back," the Scarecrow said. "Take me first. If I fall, the rocks won't hurt me."

"If I fall, I will be killed," the Lion replied. "That makes me very afraid. But get on my back. I will try to jump across."

So the Scarecrow got on the Lion's back and the animal did a great jump. When he landed safely on the other side, the Tin Man and Dorothy shouted happily.

The Lion jumped back for Dorothy and Toto.

"Hold on!" the Cowardly Lion cried and he jumped again.

When Dorothy was safe on the other side, the Lion went back for the Tin Man. Then the huge animal had to rest.

The forest was dark now, but the yellow brick road went on.

"Will this forest never end?" Dorothy asked sadly.

They walked on and soon they came to another ditch.

"I'm sorry, but I can't jump that. It is too wide," the Cowardly Lion said. "What can we do now?"

"I have an idea," the Scarecrow said at last. "Look, there is a tall tree next to the ditch. If the Tin Man cuts the tree down, it will fall across the ditch like a bridge. Then we can all walk across to the other side."

"That is a great idea," the Lion said.

The Tin Man picked up his axe and began to work at once. He chopped[41] at the tree for some time. When it was ready to fall, the Lion pushed the tree hard and it fell across the ditch. Now they could all walk to the other side.

Dorothy went first, with Toto in her arms. The Tin Man followed, then the Scarecrow. The Lion came last of all.

Dorothy was very tired so the Lion carried her on his back.

6

The River

In the afternoon, they came to the end of the forest. There was a wide river in front of them. On the other side of the river were beautiful green fields which were covered with flowers. The yellow brick road went on through the fields. On each side of the road there were trees too, with many kinds of fruit.

"Oh dear, how can we cross this river?" Dorothy asked.

"That's easy," the Scarecrow replied. "The Tin Man must make us a raft[42]. Then we can all float[43] across it."

The Tin Man started work. He chopped down some small trees and joined pieces of wood together. The Tin Man was a good woodman and he worked very hard. But night came before the raft was finished. So they all went to sleep under the trees. Dorothy dreamed of the Emerald City and of the Great Wizard of Oz. She dreamed that Oz was sending her home to Kansas.

When Dorothy woke up, she immediately saw that she was not in Kansas. But she felt happy now, because the dark forest was behind them. The girl picked some fruit for her breakfast and washed her face. Then she was ready.

The Tin Man had finished the raft and they were ready to start. When the raft was in the water, Dorothy sat down on it, with Toto in her arms. Then, very carefully, the Lion got on too. He was very heavy and the raft moved up and down.

The Scarecrow and the Tin Man had long poles. They stood at the end of the raft and they held it steady. Then they slowly began to push the raft along with their poles.

At first, everything went well. But in the middle of the river the water was moving very fast. It was deeper there too. The water carried them further and further away from the yellow brick road.

"This is very bad," said the Tin Man. "The river is carrying us into the country of the Wicked Witch of the West. She might catch us!"

"Then I will never have brains," said the Scarecrow sadly.

"And I will never have courage," said the Cowardly Lion.

"And I will never have a heart," said the Tin Man.

"And Toto and I will never get back to Kansas," said Dorothy, and she began to cry.

"Please don't cry, my dear," the Scarecrow said kindly. "We must try to get to the Wizard, if we can."

Then he pushed very hard on his long pole. The raft moved very fast, but without the poor Scarecrow. He was left holding his pole, in the middle of the river!

"Goodbye," the Scarecrow shouted to his friends on the raft. "Good luck!" Then he thought to himself, "I will never have any brains now. When Dorothy found me, I was on a pole in a field. Now I am on a pole in the middle of the river and no one can help me."

The raft floated on. Soon the Scarecrow was left far behind.

"I have an idea," the Cowardly Lion said to the Tin Man. "I think that I can swim to the river bank[44]. Hold onto my tail. Then I will pull the raft after me."

So the Lion jumped into the water and started to swim. The Tin Man stood on the raft and held onto the Lion's tail. Dorothy pushed with the Tin Man's long pole. Very slowly, the raft moved nearer to the land.

At last they were on the river bank and they sat on the green grass to rest.

"What must we do now?" the Tin Man asked Dorothy.

"We must get back to the yellow brick road," the girl replied. "If we don't, we'll never find the Emerald City."

"If we walk back along the river bank, we'll come to the road again," the Lion said. "Let me get dry under the sun. Then we can start."

So they all rested and looked at the beautiful country around them. Dorothy was almost happy again. But then she thought of the poor Scarecrow and she felt very sad.

"Let's go," the Tin Man said at last and they started off. Soon they saw the Scarecrow in the middle of the river.

"We can't leave him standing there. How can we save him?" Dorothy asked her friends. But no one knew how to save the poor Scarecrow.

At that moment, a big bird called a Stork flew by. When the Stork saw the friends, he stopped.

"Hello," he said to them. "Who are you and where are you going? I have never seen people like you before."

"I am Dorothy," the girl said. "This is my dog, Toto. This Tin Man and the Cowardly Lion are my friends. We are all going to the Emerald City, to see the Wizard of Oz."

"You should be on the yellow brick road," the Stork said.

"Yes, we know," Dorothy replied. "But that Scarecrow in the river is our friend. He wants to go with us, but we can't reach him."

The Stork looked across at the Scarecrow.

"I can carry things," he said. "But he is too heavy for me."

"Oh, no, he is not heavy at all," Dorothy said quickly. "He is made of straw. Oh, please do try to help him!"

"Well," the Stork said, "I will try."

So the Stork flew slowly across the water and picked up the Scarecrow easily. Then he flew back to the bank.

The Scarecrow was so happy that he hugged[45] everyone.

"Thank you for helping me," the Scarecrow said to the Stork. "If I ever get brains, I'll come back and help you too."

"That's all right," the Stork said. "I hope that you find the Emerald City. Get back to the yellow brick road as soon as you can."

"Yes, we will," Dorothy said. Then the Stork flew slowly away.

7

The Field of Sleep

The friends walked as fast as they could. As they walked, they looked at all the beautiful things around them. Brightly colored birds were flying about and singing in the trees. The ground was covered with yellow, white, blue and purple flowers. There were lots of bright-red poppies too.

"The poppies are the most beautiful flowers," Dorothy said. "They are so bright and their scent[46] is beautiful."

"I have always loved flowers," said the Cowardly Lion. "But these are more beautiful than the ones in the forest."

"I would like them more, if I had brains," said the Scarecrow.

"And I would love them too, if I had a heart," said the Tin Man.

There were more and more poppies now. Their scent was very strong and Dorothy began to feel sleepy. Toto was sleepy too. Dorothy was in danger, but she did not know it. If she fell asleep in the poppy field, she might never wake up again.

"I'm very tired," Dorothy said. "I must sleep."

"No, you can't sleep here, my dear," the Tin Man told her.

"We must get back to the yellow brick road before dark."

But it was too late. Dorothy's eyes had closed.

"What shall we do?" the Tin Man asked.

"If we leave her here, she will never wake again," the Lion replied. "You are safe, but I'm made of flesh. I'm becoming sleepy too."

"Then run as fast as you can," the Scarecrow said to the Lion. "The Tin Man and I will carry Dorothy and Toto out of the field. But we can't carry you! Go quickly!"

The Cowardly Lion began to run through the poppy field and the friends carried the girl and her dog between them.

They walked on through the poppies. Near the end of the field, they found the Cowardly Lion. He was fast asleep.

"We can't carry him. He is too heavy," the Tin Man said sadly. "He will sleep here for ever. Perhaps he will dream that he has courage."

"I'm sorry to leave him," the Scarecrow replied. "He was a coward, but he was a good friend. He helped us all."

Dorothy and Toto were fast asleep too. The Scarecrow and the Tin Man carried them out of the poppy field and put them down on the grass. Then they waited for Dorothy to wake up.

8

The Queen of the Field Mice

"We must be near the yellow brick road now," the Scarecrow said. But before the Tin Man could reply, a little gray field mouse[47] ran by. It was followed by a yellow wildcat. The Wildcat's mouth was open.

The Tin Man had no heart, but he felt very sorry for the little mouse.

"Stop!" he cried, and he raised his axe. As the Wildcat ran by, the Tin Man cut off its head and killed it.

The little field mouse stopped. Then it slowly moved toward the Tin Man.

"Thank you," said the mouse. "You have saved a Queen!"

"A Queen? But you are a mouse!" the Tin Man said.

"I am the Queen of all the field mice," the mouse replied. "I and all my people thank you."

As she spoke, several other field mice ran up and bowed.

"We are so glad that you are safe!" they cried to their Queen.

"This Tin Man killed the Wildcat and saved my life," the Queen told them. "Now you must all do whatever he wants."

"We will!" all the field mice cried.

"Well," the Queen said to the Tin Man. "What can we mice do for you?"

"I can't think of anything . . . " the Tin Man began, but then the Scarecrow had an idea.

"You can help our friend, the Cowardly Lion," he said. "He is asleep in the poppy field."

"A lion?" cried the Queen. "If he wakes up, he'll eat us!"

"Oh, no," the Scarecrow said. "This Lion is a coward and he would never hurt our friends. Please help us to save him."

"What can we do?" the Queen asked. "We are small, but there are thousands of us field mice."

"Then tell all the mice that they must come here. Each mouse must bring a long piece of string[48]," the Scarecrow said.

Then the Scarecrow spoke to his friend, the Tin Man.

"Cut down some trees and make a truck[49], with wooden wheels. The truck must be big enough to carry the Lion."

The Tin Man began work at once. When the mice arrived, the flat wooden truck was ready.

There were thousands and thousands of mice now. Each one had a long piece of string in its mouth.

At about this time, Dorothy woke up from her sleep. She

was very surprised to find herself on the ground, with thousands of gray field mice looking at her. Then the Scarecrow explained everything and Dorothy smiled.

The Scarecrow told the mice his plan. Every field mouse had a piece of string. One end of each piece of string was tied to the truck. Then the other end was put around the neck of a mouse. Now the mice could pull the truck along. They pulled the truck to where the Lion was sleeping.

The Tin Man and the Scarecrow pushed the Lion onto the truck. He was very heavy and that took time.

All the mice pulled as hard as they could. Very slowly, the truck began to move. The Tin Man and the Scarecrow pushed the truck from behind.

Slowly, the mice pulled the Cowardly Lion out of the poppy field. Then Dorothy thanked them all for saving her dear friend from death. The string was taken from the necks of the mice and they all ran quickly away. Only the Queen stayed.

The Queen gave Dorothy a little whistle[50].

"Blow this whistle if you need our help again," she said to Dorothy. "We will come at once. Goodbye!"

"Goodbye," said the Tin Man, the Scarecrow and Dorothy. Then the Queen ran away too. The friends sat down and waited for the Lion to wake up.

9

The Emerald City

The Cowardly Lion slept for a long time. But at last he woke up and looked around him.

"I am very happy to see you all again," he said when he saw his friends. "How did you get me out of the poppy-field?"

"Well, we had some help," the Scarecrow said.

Dorothy told the Lion about the field mice and how they had saved him.

The Cowardly Lion laughed.

"I have been happy because I'm so big and strong," he said. "But little flowers nearly killed me and little animals saved me. I must remember that. What will we do now?"

"We must find the yellow brick road again," Dorothy said. "When you are ready, we will be on our way."

"I feel fine," the Lion said. "On to the Emerald City!"

Soon they reached the yellow brick road again and started walking along it.

There were houses and farms on either side of the road

now. The houses were painted green. Sometimes they saw people and they were all dressed in green too.

"This must be the Land of Oz," Dorothy said. "Everything is green, so the Emerald City can't be far away."

"I don't think that we shall get there tonight," the Scarecrow said. "We need somewhere to stay."

"Then let's stop at the next house," Dorothy said. "I want somewhere to sleep. I am feeling hungry too, and so is Toto.

Soon, they came to a farmhouse and Dorothy knocked on the door. It opened and a woman looked out.

"What do you want?" she asked. "Why is there a lion with you? He is very big and I am afraid of him."

"Please don't worry. This is the Cowardly Lion and he is more afraid of you," Dorothy replied. "He is my friend and so is this Scarecrow and this Tin Man. Can we all stay with you tonight? We have walked a long way."

"Come in," the woman said. "You can have some supper too."

There was a man in the house. He looked up in surprise when Dorothy and her friends entered.

"Where are you all going?" the man asked.

"To the Emerald City, to see the Great Oz," Dorothy replied.

"Are you sure that Oz will see you?" the man said. "I have been there many times, but I have never seen him."

"Why not?" the Scarecrow asked.

"He never goes out," the man replied. "He stays in his palace every day."

"What does the Great Oz look like?" Dorothy asked.

"That is a difficult question," the man replied. "Oz is a great Wizard, so he can change himself by magic. No one is sure what he looks like. He never sees anyone."

"Oh dear," Dorothy said. "We have come a long way to see him. We all want him to help us, you see."

"Yes, I want Oz to give me some brains," said the Scarecrow.

"I want a heart," said the Tin Man.

"And I want courage," said the Cowardly Lion.

"Oh, all those things will be easy for him," the man replied. Then he turned to Dorothy.

"And what do you want, my dear?" he asked.

"I want Oz to send me and Toto back to Kansas," she replied.

"I have never heard of Kansas," the man said. "Is it far?"

"I don't know. But I know that it is my home and that I want to go back there," Dorothy explained sadly.

"I'm sure that Oz knows where Kansas is. He knows everything," the man said. "But you will have to see him first and that will be difficult."

The woman gave them supper—though the Scarecrow and the Tin Man did not eat anything. Then Dorothy and Toto went to sleep on a soft bed and the Lion slept by the door.

The Scarecrow and the Tin Man stood up all night.

In the morning, they all thanked the man and woman and started on their way. There was a green light shining in the sky.

"That must be the Emerald City," Dorothy said.

They walked all day. The green light in the sky got brighter and brighter. In the afternoon, they came to the end of the yellow brick road. It ended at the high green wall that went around the Emerald City.

In front of them was a big gate. It was covered with emeralds[51]. The beautiful green stones shone in the sunlight.

Dorothy rang the bell beside the gate. It opened and they walked into a beautiful room. Everything shone with a green light.

A little green man stood in the middle of the room.

"You are entering the Emerald City" the green man said. "I am the Guardian[52] of the Gate. Can I help you?"

"We have come to see the Great Oz," Dorothy replied.

The green man looked very surprised.

"No one has asked to see Oz for years," he said. "He is a very great Wizard, but he is terrible too. If you have come here to waste his time[53], he will be very angry. You may never leave the Emerald City again."

"We were told that Oz was a good Wizard," the Scarecrow said. "We've come a long way. We haven't come here to waste his time."

"Then I will take you to his Palace," the green man said.

The Emerald City of Oz was a wonderful place. All the buildings were made of green marble[54], with windows made of green glass. There were beautiful green emeralds everywhere.

All the people were green and they were wearing green clothes too. The green people looked at Dorothy and her friends as they walked by. But no one spoke to them.

At last, the friends came to a big building in the middle of the city. It was the Palace of Oz, the Great Wizard. A soldier, dressed in green, was standing in front of the door.

"These people are strangers," the Guardian of the Gate said to the soldier. "They want to see the Great Oz."

The soldier looked surprised.

"Come in," he said. "I will tell Oz that you are here." Then the soldier went away for a long time.

"Did you see Oz?" Dorothy asked, when he came back.

"Oh, no. I have never seen him," the soldier replied. "He sits behind a screen[55]. But I told him about you."

"And what did he say?" the Tin Man asked.

"Oz will see you, but not all together. He will speak to one of you every day." the soldier replied. "Now you can go to your rooms. You can rest there, until Oz sends for you."

At last the friends came to a big building in the middle of the city. It was the Palace of Oz, the Great Wizard.

"Thank you," Dorothy said. "That is very kind of Oz."

A girl dressed in green, with beautiful green hair and green eyes, came into the room and smiled at Dorothy.

"Please follow me," the girl said. Then Dorothy, with Toto in her arms, followed her through the Palace of the Great Oz.

The green girl opened a door that was covered with emeralds.

"Here you are," she said to Dorothy. "You will be happy here. Sleep well and Oz will send for you tomorrow morning. Now I must take your friends to their rooms."

Everything in Dorothy's room was green. The soft bed was covered in green. There were green dresses for Dorothy to wear and green books for her to read.

Dorothy slept very well that night. In the morning, after breakfast, she washed and put on a green silk dress. She tied a green ribbon[56] around Toto's neck. They were ready.

10

The Great Wizard of Oz

The next morning, the green girl came for Dorothy. Oz had asked to see the girl and her little dog.

"Oz does not usually see people," the green girl explained. "But the soldier told him about your Silver Shoes. The Great Oz was very interested. He will see you now, in his Throne Room[57]. I think that you are very brave, my dear."

The Throne Room was round and high and very big. Everything in it was covered in shining emeralds.

Oz's green throne stood in the middle of the room. On the throne was a Huge Head. There was no body, no arms and no legs. The Head had no hair, but it had two eyes, a nose and a mouth. The mouth opened and Oz spoke.

"I am Oz, the Great and the Terrible," he said. "Who are you?"

"I am Dorothy, the Small and the Quiet," the girl replied.

"Where did you get those Silver Shoes?" the Wizard asked.

"From the Wicked Witch of the East," Dorothy replied. "My house fell on her and killed her."

"The Good Witch of the North has kissed you," the Great Oz said slowly. "I can see her mark."

"Yes, then she sent me to you, Great Oz," Dorothy replied.

"You have had a long journey. Why are you here?" Oz asked. "What do you want me to do?"

"Please send me back to my Aunt Em and Uncle Henry in Kansas," Dorothy said quickly. "You have a beautiful country, but it is not my home. I have been away from Kansas for so long. I do so want to go home!"

"Why do you need my help?" Oz asked. "You killed the Wicked Witch of the East all by yourself."

"That was a mistake," Dorothy replied.

"I see," Oz said. "Well, I will help you. But you must also help me."

"What can I do for you?" she asked in surprise.

"You must kill the Wicked Witch of the West," Oz replied.

"I don't want to kill anyone!" Dorothy cried.

"You killed the Wicked Witch of the East. You are wearing her Silver Shoes. When the Wicked Witch of the West is dead, I will send you back to Kansas," Oz said.

Dorothy began to cry.

"The Witch may be wicked, but I still don't want to kill her," she told Oz. "I am only a girl and you are Oz, the Great and the Terrible. Why don't you kill her yourself?"

"You have my answer," Oz replied. "If you don't kill the Wicked Witch, you'll never see your aunt and uncle again!"

Dorothy went back to her friends and told them everything.

"I shall never get back to Kansas now," she said sadly.

Her friends were very sorry, but they could not help her. Dorothy went back to her green room with Toto. Then she lay down on the green bed and cried until she fell asleep.

The next morning, the Scarecrow was taken to see Oz.

"I must not be afraid of a Head," the Scarecrow said to himself, as he walked into the Throne Room. Dorothy had told the Scarecrow about her meeting with Oz the day before. She had explained that Oz was a Head with no hair, two eyes, a nose and a mouth.

But when the Scarecrow looked up he saw, not a Head, but a beautiful Woman sitting on the throne. She was dressed in green and her hair was green too. She had two huge wings[58] that moved all the time.

"Who are you?" the Scarecrow asked in surprise.

"I am Oz, the Great and the Terrible," the Green Woman said. "Who are you? And why are you here?"

"I am a Scarecrow, I am stuffed with straw," the Scarecrow said. "I would like to have brains in my head, instead of straw."

"I can give you brains," said the Green Woman. "I am the Great Oz and I can do anything. But first you must do something for me. I want you to kill the Wicked Witch of the West."

"But you asked Dorothy to kill the Witch!" the Scarecrow replied.

"I don't care who kills the Witch," Oz told the Scarecrow. "But you will have no brains until she is dead. You can go now."

The Scarecrow was very sad. He went back to his friends and told them everything. The next morning, it was the Tin Man's turn to see the Wizard.

When the Tin Man saw the Great Oz, he was very afraid. This time, the Great Wizard was a Huge Animal. The Huge Animal had five eyes, five arms and five legs. It was covered in long hair. It was much bigger than the Cowardly Lion.

"I am Oz, the Great and the Terrible," the Huge Animal roared. "Who are you and why are you here?"

"I am a woodman," the Tin Man said. "As you can see, I

am made of tin and so I have no heart. Please give me a heart, Great Oz. Then I can love and be happy."

"First you must kill the Wicked Witch of the West," the Huge Animal roared. "Then I will give you a heart."

"Well, it will be my turn tomorrow," the Cowardly Lion said when the Tin Man had returned to his friends. "I am ready for the Head, the Green Woman or the Huge Animal. I will roar and the Great Oz will be afraid of me."

But when the Cowardly Lion saw Oz, he had a surprise. This time, the Great Wizard was a Ball of Fire, hot and bright. The Cowardly Lion was very afraid.

"I am Oz, the Great and the Terrible," the Ball of Fire roared. "Who are you and why are you here?"

"I'm the Cowardly Lion and I'm always afraid," the Lion said. "Please give me courage so I can be King of the animals."

The Ball of Fire became hotter and hotter and the Cowardly Lion had to move further away.

"When the Wicked Witch of the West is dead, I will give

you courage," the Wizard said. "What do you think of that?"

The Cowardly Lion was too afraid to answer. He ran back to his friends and told them everything.

"What can we do now?" Dorothy asked sadly.

"We must find the Wicked Witch and kill her," the Cowardly Lion said. "If we don't, I will never have courage."

"And I will never have brains," said the Scarecrow.

"And I will never have a heart," said the Tin Man.

"And I will never see Aunt Em and Uncle Henry again," said Dorothy. And her tears fell onto her beautiful green dress.

"Don't cry, you'll spoil your dress," the Tin Man told her.

So Dorothy stopped crying and said,

"We must find the Witch, but I don't want to kill her."

"I'll go with you, but I *am* a coward," the Lion replied.

"I have no brains, but I will go with you," the Scarecrow said.

"I don't want to kill anyone, but I will go with you too," the Tin Man said. "We'll all go together and find the Wicked Witch."

"We'll go tomorrow," Dorothy said, and Toto barked loudly.

11

The Wicked Witch of the West

The friends got up early the next morning and had a good breakfast. The green girl filled Dorothy's basket with food. Then the green soldier took them back to the gate.

"Which road will take us to the Wicked Witch of the West?" Dorothy asked the Guardian of the Gate.

"There isn't a road," he replied. "No one goes that way."

"How can we find her then?" Dorothy asked.

The Guardian of the Gate laughed.

"Don't worry. The Wicked Witch will find you!" he told her. "And when she finds you, she will make you her slaves[59]."

"But we are going to kill her," said the Scarecrow.

"The Witch may not let you kill her," the Guardian of the Gate explained. "She is very wicked and she may kill *you*. But if you want to find her, follow the sun and walk towards the West."

So the friends began to walk towards the West and away from the Emerald City. Soon, Dorothy's green dress turned white and Toto's green ribbon went white too.

As they went on, walking became difficult. The ground was hard and there were no farms or houses. The sun was hot and there were no trees. Dorothy, Toto and the Lion soon became very tired. They fell asleep before it was dark and the Scarecrow and the Tin Man stood near them.

The Wicked Witch of the West had only one eye, but she could see everything. She saw Dorothy first. The girl was fast asleep, with her friends all around her.

The Wicked Witch was very angry and she blew on her silver whistle. Almost at once, a pack of wolves[60] ran towards her. The animals had long legs, red eyes and sharp teeth.

"Go and tear[61] those strangers into pieces!" the Wicked Witch told the Leader of the wolves.

"Don't you want to use them for slaves?" the Leader of the wolves asked.

"No, they are no use to me," the Wicked Witch replied. "One is made of tin and one of straw. The girl and the lion won't be able to work for me. Tear them into pieces."

"We will!" the Leader said and the wolves all ran towards the strangers.

The Scarecrow and the Tin Man saw the wolves coming.

"Leave this to me," the Tin Man said, and he raised his axe. As the Leader of the wolves ran up, the Tin Man swung his axe. The wolf's head was cut from its body.

There were forty wolves. The Tin Man raised his axe forty times. Forty heads were cut off and all the wolves were dead. Then the Tin Man sat down and smiled.

"That was a good fight," he said to the Scarecrow.

When Dorothy woke up in the morning, she saw the wolves' heads and bodies all around her. At first, she was afraid, but then the Tin Man told the girl everything.

"Thank you for saving my life," she replied. Then she hugged him.

After a good breakfast, the friends started on their way.

The Wicked Witch looked out of the door of her castle. First, she saw all the dead wolves. Then she saw the strangers walking through her country and she was very, very angry. The Witch blew her silver whistle and a flock[62] of black crows flew towards her.

"Peck[63] out the strangers' eyes! Tear them to pieces!" the Wicked Witch said to the King Crow.

"Right!" the King Crow replied.

When Dorothy saw the black crows coming she was very afraid.

"Don't worry," the Scarecrow said. "Leave this to me."

When the crows saw the Scarecrow, at first they were afraid of him. But then the King Crow said, "He's only stuffed with straw. I will peck his eyes out."

The King Crow flew down, but the Scarecrow caught him. He twisted the bird's neck until it was dead.

One by one, the crows flew at the Scarecrow. He caught each one and twisted its neck. Soon, the forty black crows were dead.

"You are safe now," the Scarecrow said to his friends. And they started on their way again.

When the Wicked Witch saw the dead crows, she was more angry than before. She blew three times on her silver whistle and a swarm[64] of black bees came flying towards her.

"Sting[65] those strangers to death!" she cried. "Be quick!"

But the Scarecrow saw the bees coming and he knew what to do.

"Take out my straw and cover the girl, the dog and the Lion with it," the Scarecrow said to the Tin Man. "Then the bees can't sting them."

So when the bees came, there was only the Tin Man to sting. But when they flew at him, the bees broke their stings[66] and they all died.

Then Dorothy and the Lion got up. They helped the Tin Man put the straw back into the Scarecrow and they all started on their way again.

The Wicked Witch was so angry that she jumped up and down. Then she called the Winkies, who were her slaves. She gave them sharp spears[67] to fight with.

"Go and kill those strangers," she said. "Don't come back until they are dead—or I will kill you!"

The Winkies did not like fighting, but they were afraid of the Wicked Witch. They soon found Dorothy and her friends. But when the Cowardly Lion roared, the Winkies were very afraid and they ran back to the Witch's castle.

The Wicked Witch was very angry because all her plans were going wrong. She beat the Winkies and gave them a lot of hard work to do in her castle. Then she sat down and thought hard.

Soon, she had an idea. The Wicked Witch had a magic Golden Cap. The owner of the Golden Cap could ask for the help of the Winged Monkeys. The Winged Monkeys would help three times and three times only. Then the magic would stop working. The Wicked Witch had already used the Golden Cap twice.

"I will use the Golden Cap for the third time," the Wicked Witch said to herself. "The Winged Monkeys will kill these strangers for me, I am sure of that."

12

In the Power of the Wicked Witch

So the Wicked Witch put on the Golden Cap and said some magic words. Immediately, the Winged Monkeys were all around her. The Monkeys had long hairy legs and arms, evil[68] faces, and big wings.

"You have called us for the third and final time," the King of the Winged Monkeys said. "What do you want us to do?"

"Go and find the strangers in my land," the Wicked Witch told him. "Kill them all except the Lion. He can work for me."

"We will find them at once," the King replied.

The Winged Monkeys flew off[69], laughing and talking. They soon found Dorothy and her friends. Some of the Monkeys picked up the Tin Man and dropped him on some sharp rocks. The poor Tin Man's body was badly damaged[70]. Other Monkeys caught the Scarecrow and pulled out all his straw. They carried his clothes and dropped them on top of a tall tree.

Then three or four Winged Monkeys tied up the Cowardly Lion with a thick rope. They carried him back to the Witch's castle.

The King of the Monkeys looked at Dorothy and he saw the mark of the Good Witch's kiss.

"We cannot kill the girl," he told the other Monkeys. "She is protected by the Power of Good. The Power of Good is stronger than the Power of Evil. Carry her and the dog back to the castle and leave her there."

When Dorothy and Toto were outside the castle, the King of the Winged Monkeys found the Wicked Witch.

"The Tin Man and the Scarecrow are dead," he told her. "The Lion is tied up with rope. But we can't kill the girl and her dog. You have used us for the last time. Goodbye."

As the Winged Monkeys flew off, the Wicked Witch looked at Dorothy. When the Witch saw the mark of the Good Witch's kiss and the Silver Shoes, she felt afraid.

"This girl is a powerful Witch," the Wicked Witch said to herself. But then the Wicked Witch looked into Dorothy's eyes and laughed. She knew Dorothy was too simple and good to use her power.

"Come with me, my girl," the Witch said to Dorothy. "I have a lot of hard work for you to do."

Dorothy did not want to stay in the castle, but she was very glad that the Witch had not killed her. The girl began to work in the kitchen, cleaning and washing for the Wicked

Witch. Dorothy was a good girl and she worked hard. But she was very sad and she thought of her home in Kansas every day.

The Cowardly Lion was still tied up. Every time that the Wicked Witch went near him, he roared.

"I won't give you any food and you'll die!" the Witch cried. But the Cowardly Lion did not die because every night, Dorothy gave him some of her own food. Then they would talk sadly and sometimes Dorothy cried. But they could not leave the castle, because it was full of the Witch's slaves.

The Wicked Witch wanted Dorothy's Silver Shoes because she knew they had great power. But the girl loved her shoes and she always wore them. She only took them off at night, or when she had a bath.

The Wicked Witch was afraid of the dark. She was afraid of water too.

Then the Wicked Witch thought of a plan. She put a long piece of wood in the middle of the kitchen floor. Then she put magic on the wood, so that Dorothy could not see it. When Dorothy walked across the kitchen, she fell over the wood. One of her Silver Shoes came off and the Witch picked it up. The wicked old woman put the Silver Shoe on her own foot and laughed.

"Give me back my shoe!" Dorothy cried.

"It's not your shoe, it's mine now!" the Wicked Witch replied. "And I'll soon get the other one from you!"

The Witch laughed again. Dorothy was so angry that she picked up a bucket of water that stood nearby. She threw the water all over the Wicked Witch.

"Look what you have done! The water will kill me!" the Witch cried. "I am melting[71] away! Help me!"

"I'm very sorry," Dorothy said. "It was a mistake. But you made me very angry."

"And now you have killed me!" the Wicked Witch cried.

"Look what you have done! The water will kill me!" the Witch cried. "I am melting away! Help me!"

"In a few minutes, there will be nothing left of me. I am going, going, go . . ."

Dorothy looked down on the floor. The Wicked Witch had melted. There was nothing left of her but the Silver Shoe.

So the girl cleaned the kitchen floor with some more water. Then she cleaned the Silver Shoe and put it on. She told the Cowardly Lion the good news and untied his rope.

"The Wicked Witch of the West is dead!" Dorothy cried.

All the Winkies ran up to her. They were laughing happily.

"The Wicked Witch is dead!" they cried. "We are free!"

13

Dorothy and the Winged Monkeys

The Winkies had been the Wicked Witch's slaves for many years. They were very happy that Dorothy had killed her.

"Is there anything that we can do for you?" one of the Winkies asked Dorothy.

"We had two good friends, a Tin Man and a Scarecrow," Dorothy replied. "Can you find them for us?"

"Of course," the Winkies replied. They looked everywhere and at last they found the Tin Man. They carried him back to the castle and showed him to Dorothy.

The Tin Man's body was rusted and bent.

"Oh, poor Tin Man," the girl said. "What can we do?"

"Some of us are tinsmiths," a Winkie told her. "We can make him like new."

So the tinsmiths worked for three days, straightening[72] and polishing[73] the Tin Man's body until he was better than before. A goldsmith made a golden handle for his axe.

The Tin Man smiled.

"Now all I want is a heart," he said.

Then Dorothy told the Winkies about the Scarecrow.

"Don't worry, we will find him," the Winkies replied.

The Winkies looked for the Scarecrow for three days. Finally, they found his blue clothes in a tree.

The Tin Man quickly chopped down the tree. Then they took the clothes back to the castle and stuffed them with clean straw. And there was the Scarecrow again!

Now all the friends were together and they spent a few happy days in the castle. But Dorothy had not forgotten Kansas and her Aunt Em.

"We must go back to Oz and remind him of his promises," she said. "Then I can get back to Kansas."

"And I will get my brains," said the Scarecrow.

"Oz will give me a heart," said the Tin Man.

"And I shall have courage at last," said the Cowardly Lion.

"Let's start for the Emerald City at once!" Dorothy cried.

The friends said goodbye to the Winkies, who were sorry to see them go. Dorothy went into the kitchen to look for some food. She saw the Golden Cap and she put it on. Now Dorothy was wearing the Silver Shoes *and* the Golden Cap, but she did not know that they were magic.

There was no road between the castle of the Wicked Witch and the Emerald City. The friends followed the sun towards the east. But when the sun was directly above them, they lost their way.

The next day was overcast[74]. They could not see the sun because it was hidden behind the clouds. Several days went by and they kept on walking through fields full of flowers. But they were no nearer to the Emerald City.

"I'll never get my brains now," said the Scarecrow sadly.

"And what about my heart?" asked the Tin Man.

"I don't have the courage to keep on walking like this," the Cowardly Lion said. "I must have a rest."

"I have an idea," Dorothy said. "I'll call the field mice!"

So the girl blew the whistle that the Queen of the field mice had given her. In a few minutes, the little mice were everywhere.

"How can we help you, my dear?" the Queen asked.

"We cannot find the Emerald City," Dorothy said.

"This is because you have been walking the wrong way," the little Queen said. "Why don't you use the magic of the Golden Cap? It is yours now. You can call the Winged Monkeys. They will carry you to the Emerald City in an hour!"

"Is the Golden Cap magic? What must I do?" the girl asked.

"The magic words are written inside the cap," the Queen said. "If you say them with the cap on your head, the Monkeys will come. They have to obey[75] you. But we will go first, because we don't like them. Goodbye!"

The Queen ran away quickly, and all the little mice followed her.

Dorothy took off the Golden Cap and looked at the words inside. When she had learned them, she put the cap back on her head. Then she said the words very loudly. The Winged Monkeys arrived almost at once.

"How can we help you?" said their King.

"Please can you take us to the Emerald City?" the girl asked.

"That's easy," the King of the Winged Monkeys replied. "We will fly you there. You are the owner of the cap now and we must obey you three times."

So the journey back to the Emerald City was easy after all.

Soon the friends could see the city's shining green walls. The Winged Monkeys put them down outside the big gate. Their King bowed to Dorothy and the Monkeys flew away.

"That was a good ride," Dorothy said.

"And a quick one too," the Cowardly Lion said. "The Great Oz will be very surprised to see us again."

14

The Wonderful Wizard of Oz

The four friends walked up to the gate and Dorothy rang the bell. Soon, the Guardian of the Gate came out.

"So you have come back," he said. "I thought that you went to see the Wicked Witch of the West."

"We did," the Scarecrow said. "And now we are back."

"How did you get away from the Wicked Witch of the West?" the Guardian asked.

"Dorothy threw water over her and she melted," the Scarecrow explained. "That was the end of her."

"The Wicked Witch of the West is dead? That is wonderful news! Oz will be very pleased," the Guardian said. "The soldier will take you to the Palace."

As the friends walked through the Emerald City, a great crowd of people came into the streets to watch them. The people had learned that the Wicked Witch of the West was dead. They knew that Dorothy had melted her and they wanted to see the girl.

The friends were taken to their rooms in the Palace. The news about the Wicked Witch was sent to the Great Oz.

Dorothy and her friends waited for several days, but Oz did not send for them. Then the Scarecrow became tired of waiting.

"Tell Oz this," the Scarecrow said to the green girl. "Dorothy has the Golden Cap. If Oz does not see us tomorrow, Dorothy will call the Winged Monkeys. They will know what to do."

Oz was very frightened of the Winged Monkeys. He promised to see the four friends at nine o'clock the next morning.

This time, they all went into the Throne Room together. They looked around, but they could not see the Great Oz anywhere. In the room was a throne, a few chairs and a screen. Then they heard a Voice.

"I am Oz, the Great and the Terrible," the Voice said.

"Where are you, Great Oz?" Dorothy asked.

"I am everywhere," the Voice said. "What do you want?"

"You wanted me to kill the Wicked Witch," Dorothy said bravely. "Well, I have killed her. Now you must send me back to Kansas, as you promised."

"You promised me brains," said the Scarecrow.

"You promised me a heart," said the Tin Man.

"I was promised courage," said the Cowardly Lion.

"Did I make all those promises?" the Voice said. "Well, the Wicked Witch is dead! I must have time to think."

"But I want my courage NOW!" the Cowardly Lion said. "And I WILL have it!"

He was so angry that he gave a great roar. The roar was so frightening that Toto jumped away from him. The little dog knocked over the screen. Behind the screen was a little old man.

The Tin Man ran towards the man and raised his axe.

"Who are *you*?" the Tin Man cried. "Where is Oz?"

"I am Oz," the little old man said. "Please don't hit me. People think that I am a Great Wizard, but I'm only a man."

"Then you are a HUMBUG[76]," the Tin Man said. "You have told lies and deceived[77] everyone for years."

Behind the screen was a little old man.

"Yes, that's right. I am a humbug," the little old man said. "But you are the only people who know that. I know lots of tricks[78]. I tricked[79] you, didn't I?"

"Are you sorry that you tricked us?" the Scarecrow said. "Are you sorry that you are a humbug?"

"Of course I am," Oz began. "But I can't help it. Sit down and I will tell you my story. I was born in Omaha—"

"That isn't far from Kansas!" Dorothy cried.

"That's true," Oz said. "But Omaha and Kansas are both a very long way from here. When I was young, I was a balloonist[80]."

"What's a balloonist?" Dorothy asked.

"He's a man who goes up in a balloon on the day of a circus[81]," replied Oz. "People see the balloon and then they pay money to watch the animals and other things in the circus."

"Oh, yes," Dorothy said. "I saw a circus in Kansas."

"One day, I was in the balloon and the rope broke," the little man went on. "The balloon went up and up, above the clouds. It flew on for a night and a day and then the balloon came down in a beautiful country. The people were afraid of me, because I had come down from the sky. They thought that I was a Great Wizard."

"But you couldn't do any magic at all," the Scarecrow said slowly. "You were a humbug from the beginning."

"You are right," Oz said. "I told the people to build this city and they did. They built me a palace and I lived inside it. I did not want to see anyone, because I was afraid of the Witches. Two of them were good, but two of them were very bad. I was afraid of the bad Witches so I was very happy when the Wicked Witch of the East was killed."

"Then you sent us to kill the Wicked Witch of the West for you," Dorothy said.

"You promised to help us if we did," the Scarecrow said.

"That's true. But I can't keep those promises. I'm sorry."

"Then you are a very bad man," Dorothy said.

"No, I'm a good man, but a very bad Wizard," Oz replied.

"But what about my brains?" asked the Scarecrow.

"What about my heart?" asked the Tin Man.

"And what about my courage?" asked the Cowardly Lion.

"I don't think that you need these things," the Great Oz said. "But if you come to me tomorrow, I will help you."

"How am I to get back to Kansas?" Dorothy asked.

"I must think about that," Oz said. "I will try to help you too. But please don't tell anyone that I am a humbug."

The friends agreed and they went back to their rooms feeling hopeful.

The Scarecrow was the first to be called to the Great Oz.

"When I come back, I shall have brains like you," he said to Dorothy. Then he went happily into the Throne Room.

Oz was ready for the Scarecrow.

"First, I must take some straw from your head," Oz said. "Then I will give you your new brains. Sit down, please."

He took out the straw and mixed it up with pins and needles and glue[82]. Then he put it all back into the Scarecrow's head.

"There you are," Oz said. "You're as clever as anyone now."

"Thank you," the Scarecrow said. "I feel quite different."

Then it was the Tin Man's turn to see Oz.

"I've come for my heart," he said. "It will be a kind one, I hope."

"Of course. Here it is," Oz said. "First, I must cut a hole in your body, but I promise I won't hurt you."

Oz cut a piece of tin from the Tin Man's body. Then he

put a big, red, silk heart inside, and closed up the hole.

"That is a good, kind heart," Oz said. "Look after it well."

"Yes, I will and thank you very much," the Tin Man said.

Then he went back to his friends, smiling happily.

"Now it is my turn," the Lion said.

Inside the Throne Room, Oz was waiting for him.

"I have come for my courage," the Cowardly Lion said.

Oz went to a cupboard and took out a square green bottle. There was green liquid inside the bottle. Oz poured the liquid into a dish and gave it to the Lion.

"Here it is," Oz said. "You must drink it."

"It's green. What is it?" the Lion asked.

"When it's inside you, it will be courage," Oz said. "You must drink it quickly!" So the Lion drank it all.

"How do you feel now?" Oz asked.

"Full of courage!" the Lion replied, and he went happily back to his friends.

Oz sat alone in his Throne Room and he thought very carefully.

"Am I a humbug?" he asked himself. "I'm not a Wizard, because I can't do magic. But people believe that I can. I have made the Scarecrow, the Tin Man and the Lion very happy. Is there anything wrong in that? But how can I get Dorothy back to Kansas? That will be much more difficult."

Oz thought for three days and then he sent for Dorothy.

"Sit down, my dear," the little old man said to the girl. "I have found a way to get you out of the Land of Oz."

"And back to Kansas, O Great Humbug?" Dorothy asked.

"Well, I'm not sure about that," Oz replied. "You will have to cross the desert first."

"How can I do that?" Dorothy asked. "I can't fly!"

"I came here in a balloon," Oz said. "I think that we can leave in a balloon too."

"We?" Dorothy cried. "Are you coming with me?"

"Yes," Oz said. "I'll make a balloon of silk and fill it with hot air. You must help me, my dear. I am sure that you can sew[83] very well."

"Aunt Em taught me to sew, back in Kansas," Dorothy said.

"I would like to meet your Aunt Em," the little old man said. "I will fly back with you to Kansas and get work in a circus there. I am tired of being a humbug."

So Dorothy and Oz began to make a balloon from pieces of green silk. Oz cut the silk and the girl sewed the pieces together. Next, Oz covered the balloon with glue. The glue would help to keep the air inside.

A big basket was fixed to the balloon with rope. Then the balloon was carried outside the Palace of the Great Oz. All the people of the Emerald City came to look at it.

The Tin Man cut some wood and made a fire under the balloon's basket. The air inside the balloon began to get hot and it started to rise. But there was a rope holding the balloon to the ground, so it could not go up.

Oz got inside the basket and spoke to his people.

"I am going to make a visit. I will be away for a time," he said in a loud voice. "I have asked the Scarecrow to look after you. Please obey him."

The air inside the balloon was very hot now.

"Get in quickly, Dorothy!" Oz called. "It's time to go!"

"I can't find Toto!" the girl cried. "Toto, where are you?"

The little dog ran up to her but it was too late! The rope had broken and the balloon was rising[84] into the air.

"Come back! I want to go too!" Dorothy cried.

"I can't come back, my dear," shouted Oz. "Goodbye! Goodbye everyone!"

And so the Great Wizard of Oz left the Emerald City. His people never knew that he was a Great Humbug. They were very sorry to see him go.

"Get in quickly, Dorothy!" Oz called. "It's time to go!"

15

The Journey to the South

Dorothy cried for a long time after Oz left. "How will I ever get back to Kansas now?" she said. "I'll never see Aunt Em and Uncle Henry again."

"I am sorry," the Tin Man said. "Oz was a humbug, but he gave me my heart."

The friends were in the Throne Room. The Scarecrow was now the King of the Emerald City. He was sitting on the throne and the others were standing in front of him.

"I have been very lucky," the Scarecrow said. "Not long ago, I was on a pole in a field. Now I am King of this beautiful city. We can all be happy, if Dorothy can forget her home in Kansas."

"But I don't want to forget Kansas!" the poor girl cried. "I think about my home every day. I want to go back."

"Well then, we must try to help you," the Tin Man said.

The Scarecrow was thinking very hard with his new brains.

"Why don't you call the Winged Monkeys?" he asked at last. "They can carry you over the desert."

Dorothy ran to get her Golden Cap. Then she said the magic words and the Winged Monkeys arrived at once.

"This is your second wish. How can we help you?" the King of the Winged Monkeys asked.

"I want you to carry me back to Kansas," Dorothy said.

"I'm sorry. We can't do that," the King of the Winged Monkeys replied. "We can only fly in this country. Winged Monkeys never go to Kansas. Goodbye." And the King of the Winged Monkeys flew away.

"Now I have used two of the Golden Cap's wishes," Dorothy said sadly. "I have only one wish left."

The Scarecrow thought again. Then he called the green soldier into the Throne Room.

"My friend Dorothy wishes to cross the desert," the Scarecrow said to him. "How can she do that?"

"No one ever crosses the desert," the green soldier replied.

"Please think," Dorothy said. "Can anyone help me?"

"There is Glinda, the Witch of the South," the green soldier said slowly. "She is the most powerful of all the witches. She rules over the Quadlings and her castle is very near the desert. She may be able to help you."

"Is Glinda a good witch?" Dorothy asked.

"Glinda is good and kind. And she is beautiful too," the green soldier replied. "But the journey to the Land of the South is very dangerous. Quadlings never come to the Emerald City."

Then the green soldier bowed and left the Throne Room.

"So I must go to the Land of the South," Dorothy said.

"I will go with you," the Lion said. "You will need me to help you. I am a wild animal and I am tired of living in a city. I want to see the forest again."

"I will go with you," the Tin Man said. "I'll take my axe."

"When do we start?" the Scarecrow asked.

"But you are the King of the Emerald City!" his friends said. They were all speaking at the same time.

"I must help Dorothy," the Scarecrow replied. "She found me in the cornfield and brought me here."

"Thank you," Dorothy said. "You are all very kind."

The next morning, the friends left the Emerald City.

"You have all looked after me very well," Dorothy said to the Guardian of the Gate. "I will never forget my time here."

"I wish that you could stay," the Guardian replied, "but I know that Kansas is your home."

"We will do our best to help her," the Scarecrow said. "I will be back as soon as Dorothy is on her way to Kansas."

The sun was shining brightly as the friends began their journey to the Land of the South. They were all feeling very happy. Dorothy was thinking of Kansas. The Tin Man and the Scarecrow were happy because they were helping her.

The animals were happy too.

"I don't like city life at all," the Lion said as he walked along. "The forest is the best place for me."

Toto was running about and barking loudly.

The friends all stopped to take a final look at the Emerald City. It shone with a beautiful green light. In the middle of the city was the Palace of the Great Oz.

"Oz was not a bad Wizard," said the Tin Man. "He gave me my heart and I am very happy with it."

"My brains have been useful already," said the Scarecrow.

"And I am not a coward anymore," said the Lion.

Dorothy said nothing. Oz hadn't helped her at all.

On the first day of their journey, the friends walked through green fields. They slept well that night, and in the morning, they came to a forest. They walked on.

"This is a fine place for a wild animal," the Lion said. "I would like to stay here. There may be other wild animals, but I can't see any. We must look for them."

The Lion's friends were a little afraid of seeing wild animals, but they said nothing. They slept under the trees that night. The next morning, the friends heard some strange sounds, but they walked on again bravely.

After a time, they came to a big open place that was full of wild animals—there were hundreds and hundreds of them. There were tigers, elephants, bears, wolves and many others. At first, Dorothy was afraid. But the Lion told her that the animals were having a meeting.

"I think they are worried about something," he said.

At that moment, a tiger came up to the Lion.

"Welcome, O Lion," the tiger said. "We need you to bring peace to the animals in this forest."

"How can I help you?" the Lion asked.

"A terrible monster[85] has come into the forest," the tiger replied. "The monster has eight long hairy legs and it can move very quickly. But it is as big as an elephant and it eats anything. It has eaten several of us already."

"Are there any other lions in the forest?" the Lion asked.

"No, the monster has eaten them all," the tiger replied.

"If I kill the monster, will you make me your King?" the Lion asked.

"We will!" all the animals cried.

"Where is the monster now?" the Lion asked.

"In the darkest part of the forest," the tiger said. "Be careful!"

The monster was asleep when the Lion found him. Its mouth was open and the Lion could see its huge, sharp teeth. The monster had a big, ugly head and a very fat body. The head and body were joined together by a very long thin neck.

The Lion jumped onto the monster's back and he bit its head from its body. The monster's hairy legs moved for a time, then they stopped. Then the Lion went back to his friends and the other animals.

"The monster is dead. I am your King!" the Lion cried.

"You are our King!" all the animals roared.

"Thank you," the Lion replied. "First, I have to help my friend Dorothy get back to Kansas. When I have done that, I will come back to the forest and be your King. Goodbye."

All the animals bowed to the Lion.

The four friends walked on to the end of the forest. In front of them was a steep hill that was covered with big pieces of rock.

"We must climb over this hill to get to the Land of the South. I'll go first," the Scarecrow said.

They had nearly reached the first rock, when they heard someone say,

"Keep back! This hill belongs to us!"

"Who are you?" asked the Scarecrow.

A short, heavy man stepped out from behind the rock. His head was flat at the top. He had a thick neck, but no arms.

"We must go over this hill. We are going to the Land of the Quadlings and you can't stop us," the Scarecrow said.

"Oh, yes I can," the man said. As he spoke, he stretched out his neck and hit the Scarecrow hard with his flat head. The poor Scarecrow rolled down the hill.

"It isn't that easy!" the man shouted. There was the sound of more laughter from behind every rock. Then Dorothy saw that there were hundreds of Hammer-Heads[86] on the hill.

The Lion roared with anger and ran up the hill. The next moment, a Hammer-Head hit him and the Lion rolled down the hill too.

"I'm sorry," the Lion said. "He was too quick for me."

"What can we do?" Dorothy asked.

"Call the Winged Monkeys!" the Tin Man said.

"What a good idea!" Dorothy cried.

She put on the Golden Cap and said the magic words. The Winged Monkeys came at once. The King bowed to Dorothy.

"What can we do for you?" he asked.

"Please carry us to the country of the Quadlings," Dorothy said.

The Winged Monkeys picked up the four friends and carried them high over the hill. The Hammer-Heads shouted and stretched out their necks, but they could not reach them.

Very soon, Dorothy and her friends were standing in the beautiful country of the Quadlings.

"That was your third wish," the King of the Winged Monkeys said to Dorothy. "You cannot send for us again. Goodbye and good luck!"

"Goodbye and thank you!" Dorothy cried.

The country of the Quadlings looked like a rich and pleasant place. The big fields were full of corn. The roads were good and the farmhouses were all painted bright red.

Some Quadlings were working in the fields. They were short fat people and they were all smiling. Their clothes were red.

Dorothy walked up to a farmhouse and knocked at the door. A Quadling woman opened it and invited the friends inside.

When Dorothy asked for some food, the woman gave them three kinds of cake and some fresh milk.

"How far is it to the Castle of Glinda, the Good Witch of

the South?" Dorothy asked the woman.

"It's not very far," the Quadling woman replied, with a smile. "Take the road to the South and you will soon be there."

So Dorothy thanked the woman and the friends walked on to a very beautiful castle. Three girls were standing by the gates. They were dressed like soldiers, in red and gold.

"Why have you come here?" one of the girls asked Dorothy.

"To see Glinda, the Good Witch," Dorothy replied. "My name is Dorothy. My friends are the Scarecrow, the Tin Man and the Lion. And this is my dog, Toto."

The girl smiled and went into the castle. In a few moments, she came out again.

"Glinda will see you at once," she said. "Come in."

16

Home Again

The girl in red took them into a big room. The Good Witch Glinda was waiting for them on her throne. She was young and beautiful. She was dressed in white and she had red hair and blue eyes. She smiled kindly at Dorothy.

"What can I do for you, my dear?" she said.

Dorothy told the Witch her story. She told her about the cyclone which carried her to the Land of Oz. She told her about meeting the Scarecrow, the Tin Man and the Lion, and all the things they had done together.

"Now I want to get back to Kansas and see my dear Aunt Em again," Dorothy said. "She doesn't know where I am. She must be very worried about me."

The Good Witch Glinda smiled and she kissed the girl.

"You have a loving heart, my dear," she said. "I can get you to Kansas. But first you must give me the Golden Cap."

"Of course I will," Dorothy replied. "I have had my three wishes. You can send for the Winged Monkeys now."

The girl took off the Golden Cap and gave it to the Good Witch Glinda. Then the Witch spoke to the Scarecrow.

"What will you do when Dorothy goes home?" Glinda asked.

"I will go back to the Emerald City," the Scarecrow replied. "Oz made me its King. But first I have to cross the hill of the Hammer-Heads."

"I will tell the Winged Monkeys to carry you back to the Emerald City," Glinda said. "You will be a good King."

Then Glinda spoke to the Tin Man.

"And what will you do?" she asked.

"I would like to return to the Country of the West," he said. "I want to be King of the Winkies."

"Then I will tell the Winged Monkeys to carry you back to the West. You will be a good King too," Glinda said.

Then Glinda smiled at the big Lion.

"What about you?" she asked. "Where will you live?"

"On the other side of the Hill of the Hammer-Heads, there is a great forest," the Lion answered. "The animals of the forest want me to be their King. I'd be very happy there."

"The Winged Monkeys will carry you there and that will be my last wish," Glinda said. "I will give the Golden Cap to the King of the Winged Monkeys. Then they will be free."

The three friends thanked the Good Witch for her kindness.

"How can I get back to Kansas?" Dorothy asked her.

"Your Silver Shoes will carry you there," the Good Witch replied. "They have powerful magic, but you did not know about it. You were able to go back to your Aunt Em as soon as you put the Silver Shoes on."

'Knock the shoes together three times and say where you want to go,' Glinda told Dorothy.

"But then I would still be in the cornfield," the Scarecrow said. "And I wouldn't have my brains."

"I have a heart now," the Tin Man said. "Dorothy helped me to leave the forest. I am very happy."

"I am happy too," the Lion said. "I am not a coward anymore and I will be King of the animals."

"I am very glad that I helped you," Dorothy said. "You have helped me too. But now I want to go back to Kansas."

"The Silver Shoes will take you there," Glinda told Dorothy. "Knock the shoes together three times and say where you want to go."

"But first I must say goodbye to my friends!" the girl said.

Then Dorothy, who was crying now, hugged the Lion and kissed him. She kissed the Tin Man and hugged the Scarecrow.

Glinda gave the girl a goodbye kiss.

Then, with Toto in her arms, Dorothy closed her eyes and knocked the Silver Shoes together three times.

"Take me home to Aunt Em, in Kansas!" Dorothy cried.

Immediately, she flew through the air, around and around, up and up. Then she quickly hit the ground with a bump. When she opened her eyes, she was sitting in front of the new house that Uncle Henry had built on the prairie. And there was Uncle Henry! Toto ran up to him, barking loudly.

Dorothy looked at her feet, but the Silver Shoes had gone. They had fallen off in the desert and were never seen again.

Aunt Em came out of the house and saw Dorothy.

"My dearest child!" she cried. "Where have you come from?"

"I have come from the Land of Oz and Toto was there too," Dorothy replied. She hugged Aunt Em and kissed her.

"Oh, Aunt Em, I am so glad to be home!" she said.

Points for Understanding

1

a Three people lived in the little wooden house on the prairie. Who were they?
b What happened to the little house when the cyclone came?

2

a "*Hours later Dorothy was woken by a hard bump.*" (page 10). Where was Dorothy when she woke up?
b "*The little woman was dressed in white.*" (page 12) Who was the woman and why did she thank Dorothy?
c Why was Dorothy going to the Emerald City?
d Dorothy had some things to protect and help her. What were they?

3

a "*That's better. I can move my legs now*". (page 18). Who said this?
b How did Dorothy help him and what did he decide to do?

4

The woodman had a body made of tin. How did this happen?

5

a Toto and Dorothy were very brave when they saw the Lion. What did they do?
b In the forest, the friends crossed two wide ditches. How did they cross them?

6

a When the friends were on the raft, these things happened to them:
   1 The Scarecrow.................
   2 The Lion.................
b The Stork gives the friends some advice. What was it?

7

a Is this sentence true?
   "The poppy flowers are dangerous. When people and animals smell them, they fall asleep."
b *"We can't carry him." "He helped us all."* (page 30)
   Who said these words and who were they talking about?

8

"You have saved a Queen." (page 31)
"Blow this whistle if you need our help again." (page 33)
Who said these things and who was she speaking to?

9

a The Cowardly Lion said that he would remember two things. What were they?
b Why did Dorothy think that they were near the Emerald City?
c Some of these sentences are true and some are false. Put T or F after them.
   1 The man in the farmhouse had seen Oz many times.
   2 The man thinks that Oz knows everything.
   3 Oz sees people all the time.
   4 Oz said that he would see the friends all together.

10

a Oz was interested in two things about Dorothy. What were they?
b Why was the Cowardly Lion surprised when he saw Oz?

c Dorothy and her three friends wanted Oz to help them in different ways. How did they want him to help them?
The Scarecrow wanted......................
The Tin Man wanted...........................
The Cowardly Lion wanted...........................
Dorothy wanted............................

d Oz wanted the friends to help him too. What did he want them to do?

11

Which of these sentences are true?

a 1 The Wicked Witch of the West blew her silver whistle three times altogether.
2 Dorothy did not see the wolves coming.
3 When the Tin Man killed the Leader of the wolves, the other wolves ran away.
4 There were more crows than wolves.
5 The black bees died when the Tin Man cut off their stings.
6 The Winkies were afraid of the Witch and of the Cowardly Lion too.

b Why did the Wicked Witch decide to use her Golden Cap for the third time?

12

a The Wicked Witch told the Winged Monkeys to kill the friends. But this did not happen.
Say what happened to each of the friends. Start your sentences with the words:
The Winged Monkeys............................
The Scarecrow............................
The Tin Man............................
The Cowardly Lion............................

b The Monkeys could not hurt Dorothy and Toto. Why not?

c The Wicked Witch wanted the Silver Shoes.
1 How did she try to get them?
2 The Wicked Witch was killed. How?

13

a Why were the Winkies happy that the Wicked Witch was dead?
b What did they do to help the Tin Man and the Scarecrow?
c What did the Queen of the field mice tell Dorothy about the Golden Cap?
d Why was Dorothy's journey back to the Emerald City so easy?

14

a The Wizard of Oz did not want to see the friends at first. How did the Scarecrow change his mind?
b When Toto knocked over the screen, what did the friends see?
c Why was the great Wizard of Oz a humbug?
d Oz said that he was a good man, but a very bad wizard. Do you agree? Give some reasons for your answer.
e The Wizard left Oz in a balloon. Why didn't Dorothy go with him?

15

a The Winged Monkeys could not obey Dorothy's second wish. Why not?
b Who was Glinda?
c Why did the animals make the Lion their King?
d How did Dorothy use the third wish of the Golden Cap?

16

a Dorothy gave Glinda the Golden Cap. Glinda said that she would use her three wishes to help the friends. How? Complete these sentences:
   1 The Winged Monkeys will carry the Scarecrow..........
   2 The Winged Monkeys will take the Tin Man..........
   3 The Winged Monkeys will carry the Lion..........
b There were no wishes left for Dorothy. How did she get back to Kansas?

Glossary

1 ***wizard*** (page 5)
a male witch.

2 ***beast*** (page 6)
a dangerous or strange animal.

3 ***exotic*** (page 6)
interesting or exciting (because something is unusal or different).

4 ***Kansas*** (page 6)
Kansas is one of the the United States of America. Each state has its own government.

5 ***prairie*** (page 6)
flat country in the middle of the USA. It has grass and farmland, but few trees.

6 ***cyclone*** (page 6)
a big storm. In a *cyclone* the wind goes round in a circle.

7 ***landscape*** (page 6)
an area of land that is beautiful to look at.

8 ***brick*** (page 6)
a small block of hard clay used for building houses or roads.

9 ***scarecrow*** (page 6)
a object shaped like a person. It is put in fields by a farmer. It frightens or scares crows (big black birds) and other birds away from the corn.

10 ***tin*** (page 6)
a soft, silver-colored metal.

11 ***whistled*** – *to whistle* (page 9)
when the wind whistles, it blows strongly and makes a high sound.

12 ***roared*** – *to roar* (page 9)
made a very loud noise that went on and on.

13 ***balloon*** (page 10)
a large strong bag filled with hot air that can go high into the sky.

14 ***bump*** (page 10)
to hit something against something.

15 ***bowed*** – *to bow* (page 12)
bending your body forward to show respect.

16 ***wicked*** (page 12)
very bad / evil.

17 ***magic*** (page 12)
a strange power that makes impossible things happen. A witch has this *magical* power.
18 ***desert*** (page 13)
dry land. It is usually sandy, with few plants and very little water.
19 ***protect*** – *to protect* (page 14)
keep safe.
20 ***mark*** (page 14)
the witch's kiss turns the girl's skin a different color.
21 ***barked*** – *to bark* (page 15)
the short loud sound made by a dog.
22 ***wagged*** – *to wag* (page 15)
moved from side to side. A dog *wags* its tail when it is happy.
23 ***pole*** (page 16)
a long thin stick.
24 ***sack*** (page 16)
a large strong bag.
25 ***stuffed*** – *to stuff* (page 16)
filled very full with something soft.
26 ***straw*** (page 16)
the yellow stems of dried crops.
27 ***flesh*** (page 19)
the soft part of people or animals' bodies. *Flesh* can be skin or muscle.
28 ***axe*** (page 19)
a tool used to cut wood or chop down trees.
29 ***woodman*** (page 19)
a man who lives in a forest and cuts down trees.
30 ***joints*** (page 19)
places where two parts are connected or joined.
31 ***rusted*** (page 19)
when some metals get wet they are damaged by a red material called rust. The Tin Man's *joints rust* and he cannot move.
32 ***oil can*** (page 19)
a container for oil. Oil will make the rusted joints move again.
33 ***path*** (page 21)
a way from one place to another. People can walk along it.
34 ***tinsmiths / goldsmiths*** (page 21)
people who work with metals are called smiths. A *tinsmith* makes things of tin and a *goldsmith* makes things of gold.

35 ***cowardly*** (page 22)
a person who is a coward, is cowardly.
36 ***coward*** (page 23)
someone who is afraid to do anything difficult or dangerous.
37 ***courage*** (page 23)
if you have courage you behave bravely.
38 ***nut*** (page 24)
a dry fruit.
39 ***ditch*** (page 24)
a long deep hole.
40 ***rocks*** (page 24)
a rock is a big piece of stone.
41 ***chopped*** – *to chop* (page 25)
cut something into pieces.
42 ***raft*** (page 25)
flat pieces of wood joined together. A *raft* carries people or things on water.
43 ***float*** – *to float* (page 25)
to move on water.
44 ***river bank*** (page 27)
the land on the side of a river.
45 ***hugged*** – *to hug* (page 29)
put your arms around someone to show love or friendship.
46 ***scent*** (page 29)
a nice smell, often of a flower or perfume.
47 ***mouse*** (page 30)
a small animal with a long tail. A field mouse lives in the fields.
48 ***string*** (page 31)
a very thin rope.
49 ***truck*** (page 31)
a flat piece of wood with wheels. A *truck* is used to carry heavy things.
50 ***a whistle*** – *to whistle* (page 33)
a small tube, usually made of metal. Blow it and it whistles.
51 ***emeralds*** (page 35)
beautiful green stones, often made into jewelry. They are very valuable.
52 ***Guardian*** (page 36)
someone who guards or looks after something or somebody.

53 ***waste his time*** – *to waste time* (page 36)
using time without a good result.

54 ***marble*** (page 36)
a hard stone, often white, but of other colors too. It is used for roads and buildings.

55 ***screen*** (page 36)
a flat piece of wood or cloth that you can hide behind.

56 ***ribbon*** (page 38)
a narrow piece of colorful cloth, used to make something or someone look pretty.

57 ***Throne Room*** (page 38)
a king or great person sits on a big chair or *throne*, in the Throne Room.

58 ***wings*** (page 40)
the parts of a bird or other creature that move up and down and make it fly.

59 ***slaves*** (page 44)
people who belong to another person and work for them. They are not paid for this work.

60 ***wolves*** (page 44)
a wild animal like a dog. They live in groups or *packs*.

61 ***tear*** – *to tear* (page 44)
to pull something into small pieces.

62 ***flock*** (page 45)
a group of birds flying together is a *flock*.

63 ***peck*** – *to peck* (page 45)
a bird's beak moves quickly to bite something when it *pecks*.

64 ***swarm*** (page 46)
a lot of bees flying together is a *swarm*.

65 ***sting*** – *to sting* (page 46)
when an insect or an animal puts a sharp part of its body into you and hurts you.

66 ***sting*** (page 46)
bees have a *sting*, a sharp part of their body.

67 ***spears*** (page 46)
long weapons with a sharp metal end.

68 ***evil*** (page 47)
very, very wicked.

69 ***flew off*** – *to fly off* (page 48)
fly away to another place.

70 ***damaged*** – *to damage* (page 48)
when something is spoiled or hurt.

71 ***melting*** – *to melt* (page 49)
changing into a liquid. Ice melts and becomes water.

72 ***straightening*** – *to straighten* (page 51)
make something straight.

73 ***polishing*** – *to polish* (page 51)
make something shine.

74 ***overcast*** (page 52)
cloudy sky.

75 ***obey*** (page 53)
to do what a law or a person says you must do.

76 ***humbug*** (page 55)
someone who says things that they know are not true. A *humbug* tries to be better and more clever than he really is.

77 ***deceived*** – *to deceive* (page 55)
tell lies. Let people believe something that is not true.

78 ***trick*** (page 57)
an unfair or unpleasant thing. You use a trick to *trick* people.

79 ***tricked*** – *to trick* (page 57)
make someone believe a lie.

80 ***balloonist*** (page 57)
a person who flies in a *balloon*.

81 ***circus*** (page 57)
a show where people and animals do clever tricks. These tricks make people laugh.

82 ***glue*** (page 58)
something that holds things together.

83 ***sew*** – *to sew* (page 60)
to join pieces of cloth together with a needle and thread.

84 ***rising*** – *to rise* (page 60)
go up into the air.

85 ***monster*** (page 65)
a large and frightening creature, usually in a story and not real.

86 ***Hammer-Heads*** (page 66)
a *hammer* is a flat heavy tool, used to hit things. These people's heads look like hammers.

Exercises

Vocabulary: meanings of words from the story

Put the words and phrases in the box next to the correct definitions.

emerald brick stuff cyclone bump roar mistake
wicked brave forehead witch smile supper stream
scarecrow mark field journey invite dangerous sack
cellar Kansas prairie straw crow

1		a large flat area in central North America covered with grass and farmland but with few trees
2		a state in the central part of the USA
3		a room under a house, below ground level, often used for storage
4		a severe storm in which the wind spins in a circle; also called a *tornado* or a *whirlwind*
5		the sound made by a crowd at a football match when a goal is scored; it is the sound made by a very strong wind; it is also the sound made by a lion
6		the sound of two hard things that come together, and the sound that something hard makes when it falls to the ground
7		a woman in stories who has magical powers
8		very bad (person); evil; wanting to harm other people
9		a block used for building walls and other structures
10		a discoloured area on the surface of something

11		something that you have done wrong or have not understood correctly
12		able to deal with danger or pain without being frightened
13		when you travel from one place to another – often it means you go a long way
14		the upper part of your face between your eyes and your hair
15		a raise of the corners of your mouth when you are happy, pleased or being friendly
16		a small and narrow river
17		an area of land used for keeping animals or growing food
18		to ask someone to come to see you and to spend time with you socially
19		the last meal of the day, usually informal and at home
20		likely to harm or damage someone or something
21		an object in the shape of a man which farmers put in their fields to frighten birds away
22		a large strong bag for storing and carrying things
23		to push something soft into a space or container
24		yellow stems of dried crops such as wheat
25		a large black bird that makes a loud noise and eats farmers' crops
26		a bright green stone used in expensive jewelry

Writing: rewrite sentences

Rewrite the sentences using the words and phrases in the previous exercise to replace the underlined words.

Example	My head is filled with straw.
You write:	*My head is stuffed with straw.*

1 The witch's kiss left a red circle on Dorothy's forehead.

2 Their house was in the Kansas flatlands.

3 'There's a tornado coming,' said Uncle Henry.

4 They hid in a room under their house.

5 The house landed on the woman who made magic.

6 She was a very evil woman.

7 Oz lives in the Bright Green City.

8 It is not near here. It will be a long way to go.

9 The road is not safe.

10 They came to a small and narrow river.

11 The rich Munchkin asked them to come into his house.

12 'We are going to eat the last meal of the day,' he said.

Vocabulary: anagrams

The letters of each word are mixed up. Write the words correctly. The first one is an example.

Example	DRAWIZ *WIZARD*	a man who makes magic
1	SERMONT	a frightening creature in stories
2	KRICT	an unfair or unpleasant thing to do to someone
3	DEVICEE	tell lies; make someone believe something that is not true
4	BOYE	do what a person or a law says you must do
5	STOVECAR	grey or cloudy (sky)
6	OSLIPH	to rub something to make it shine (shoes, furniture etc)
7	TELM	what ice and snow do in the sun
8	GAMADE	to make something less good; to spoil
9	TINGS	hurt with something sharp – some insects do it, such as wasps and bees
10	VALESS	people who belong to another person and work for him without pay
11	RHONET	the seat on which a king sits
12	LEBARM	a hard stone, often white with coloured parts, used for decoration and for making statues

Grammar: syntax

Look at the example. Put words into the correct order to make sentences.

Example	They end the brick to the road came of yellow
You write:	*They came to the end of the yellow brick road.*

1 emeralds in it covered with Everything was shining

____

2 West Witch want you to kill the I of the Wicked

____

3 and times only Winged three times three would The Monkeys help

____

4 good Dorothy knew too She was her powers simple and to use

____

5 of her left Shoe was nothing There but the Silver

____

6 for years everyone lies have You told and deceived

____

7 The Emerald King was now the Scarecrow of the City

____

8 say the shoes three times together and Knock where you want to go

____

Vocabulary: group words

Match the group words with the related animals.

~~flock~~ swarm shoal crowd school pack herd pride

1	a *flock*	of birds	5	a	of cattle
2	a	of fish	6	a	of wolves/dogs
3	a	of bees	7	a	of lions
4	a	of whales	8	a	of people

Vocabulary: job words

Match the jobs with the descriptions.

~~farmer~~ carpenter tinsmith sailor woodman barber

1	a *farmer*	grows crops	4	a	works with wood
2	a	works with metal	5	a	cuts down trees
3	a	cuts hair	6	a	works on a ship

Vocabulary and Grammar: *make / do / have*

Put *make, do* or *have* in front of these words and phrases.

1		a mistake	6		an accident
2		homework	7		the washing up
3		a good time	8		a profit
4		arithmetic	9		up your mind
5		the beds	10		the flu

Vocabulary Focus: *mark* (verb and noun)

These sentences show different meanings of the word *mark*. Replace the underlined phrase in each sentence with the correct word or phrase from the box. The first one is an example.

~~dirty marks~~ mark trade-marks the best marks
X marks the spot marks marker pen marked them

Example: The small boy's hands were covered with chocolate. He left brown smudges on the walls. brown smudges = DIRTY MARKS

1 Johnnie scored 70. Jackie scored 75. Jenny scored 80. So Jenny had the highest score.

2 Our teacher writes on a whiteboard with a special pen.

3 On this treasure map, a cross shows the place where the treasure is buried.

4 Our English teacher read our essays and gave a number for each one out of ten.

5 Five gold stars (*****) is a sign of quality.

6 Our American friend has a party on 4 July, which celebrates American Independence Day.

7 Some companies, such as Mercedes, BMW and Rolls-Royce, have distinctive company symbols on their products.

Published by Macmillan Heinemann ELT
Between Towns Road, Oxford OX4 3PP
Macmillan Heinemann ELT is an imprint of
Macmillan Publishers Limited
Companies and representatives throughout the world
Heinemann is a registered trademark of Pearson Education, used under licence

ISBN 978–0–230–03050–3
ISBN 978–1–4050–8714–8 (with CD pack)

This version of *The Wizard of Oz* by L. Frank Baum was retold by
Elizabeth Walker for Macmillan Readers
First published 2007

This version first published 2007

Illustrated by Sebastian Camagajevoc
Cover illustration by Sebastian Camagajevoc

Printed in Thailand
2013 2012 2011
9 8 7 6 5

with CD pack
2012 2011 2010
10 9 8 7 6